Thoughts on
WISDOM

Thoughts on
WISDOM

TRIUMPH BOOKS
CHICAGO

ISBN 1-57243-183-0

This book is available in quantity at special discounts
for your group or organization. For more information, contact:

TRIUMPH BOOKS
644 South Clark Street
Chicago, Illinois 60605
(312) 939-3330 FAX (312) 663-3557

Book design by Graffolio.
Cover design © 1997 by Triumph Books.
Illustrations from the Dover Pictorial Archive Series,
used with permission.
Some of the properties in the photograph on the front cover
courtesy of Bloomingdale's.

Printed in the United States of America.

Contents

Introduction vii
Advice 1
Character 7
Discovery 15
Education 23
Emotion 31
Experience 39
Failure 47
Folly 53
Freedom 61
Genius 69
Ignorance 75
Ingenuity 81
Inspiration 87
Judgment 97
Principle 105
Responsibility 113
Rhetoric 121
Sense 127
Sympathy 135
Truth 143
Index 151

INTRODUCTION

The moving motive in establishing FORBES Magazine, in 1917, was ardent desire to promulgate humaneness in business, then woefully lacking. . . .

Every issue of FORBES, since its inception, has appeared under the masthead: "With all thy getting, get understanding."

Not only so, but we have devoted, all through the years, a full page to "Thoughts on the Business of Life," reflections by ancient and modern sages calculated to inspire a philosophic mode of life, broad sympathies, charity towards all. . . .

I have faith that the time will eventually come when employees and employers, as well as all mankind, will realize that they serve themselves best when they serve others most.

B. C. Forbes

ADVICE

When you talk,
you repeat what you already know;
when you listen,
you often learn something.

JARED SPARKS

———

To profit from good advice
requires more wisdom
than to give it.

CHURTON COLLINS

———

Never seem wiser or more learned
than the company you are with.
Treat your learning like a watch
and keep it hidden.
Do not pull it out to count the hours,
but give the time when you are asked.

LORD CHESTERFIELD

He is an incorrigible ass
who will never listen to others.

BALTASAR GRACIÁN

Don't follow any advice,
no matter how good,
until you feel as deeply in your spirit
as you think in your mind
that the counsel is wise.

DAVID SEABURY

If we want to utilize in the proper way
and to the fullest extent
the products of a man's intellect,
we must develop that part of man's being
that is his heart and spirit.

FERDINAND PECORA

Have you learned lessons
only of those who admired you,
and were tender with you,
and stood aside for you?
Have you not learned great lessons
from those who rejected you,
and braced themselves against you,
or disputed the passage with you?

WALT WHITMAN

He that gives good advice
builds with one hand;
he that gives good counsel
and example builds with both;
but he that gives good admonition
and bad example
builds with one hand
and pulls down with the other.

FRANCIS BACON

None is so perfect
that he does not need at times
the advice of others.

BALTASAR GRACIÁN

———◆———

Many receive advice,
only the wise profit from it.

SYRUS

———◆———

To accept good advice
is but to increase one's own ability.

JOHANN WOLFGANG VON GOETHE

———◆———

One cool judgment
is worth a thousand hasty counsels.

WOODROW WILSON

Harsh counsels have no effect;
they are like hammers
which are always repulsed by the anvil.

HELVETIUS

One can advise comfortably
from a safe port.

FRIEDRICH VON SCHILLER

Ninety percent of all human wisdom
is the ability to mind your own business.

ROBERT A. HEINLEIN

If a man knows where to get good advice,
it is as though he could supply it himself.

JOHANN WOLFGANG VON GOETHE

CHARACTER

A man doesn't begin to attain wisdom
until he recognizes
he is no longer indispensible.

RICHARD E. BYRD

What I am thinking and doing day by day
is resistlessly shaping my future—
a future in which there is no expiation
except through my own better conduct.
No one can live my life for me.
If I am wise I shall begin today
to build my own truer
and better world from within.

H. W. DRESSER

Every generation,
no matter how paltry its character,
thinks itself much wiser
than the one immediately preceding it,
let alone those that are more remote.

WILLIAM SHAKESPEARE

———

When we know how to read our own hearts,
we acquire wisdom of the hearts of others.

DENIS DIDEROT

———

The height of human wisdom
is to bring our tempers down
to our circumstances,
and to make a calm within,
under the weight
of our greatest storm without.

DANIEL DEFOE

The force, the mass of character,
mind, heart, or soul
that a man can put into any work
is the most important factor in that work.

A. P. PEABODY

Character development is the great,
if not the sole, aim of education.

O'SHEA

The difference between a "wise guy"
and a wise man is plenty!

GALEN STARR ROSS

The wise man will want to be
ever with him
who is better than himself.

PLATO

Such is the nature of men
that howsoever they may
acknowledge many others
to be more witty, or more eloquent,
or more learned,
yet they will hardly believe
there may be many so wise as themselves.

THOMAS HOBBES

Words may show a man's wit,
but actions his meaning.

BENJAMIN FRANKLIN

As a solid rock is not shaken
by a strong gale,
so wise persons remain unaffected
by praise or censure.

BUDDHA

The desire for fame
is the last weakness
wise men put off.

TACITUS

A wise man
should have money in his head,
but not in his heart.

JONATHAN SWIFT

Wise men,
though all laws were abolished,
would lead the same life.

ARISTOPHANES

Heads are wisest
when they are cool
and hearts are strongest
when they beat in response
to noble ideals.

RALPH J. BUNCHE

The growth of wisdom
may be gauged accurately
by the decline of ill temper.

FRIEDRICH W. NIETZSCHE

Silence is the answer
to a wise man.

EURIPIDES

DISCOVERY

Reason unites us,
not only with our contemporaries,
but with men who lived
two thousand years before us,
and with those
who will live after us.

LEO TOLSTOI

Nothing is a waste of time
if you use the experience wisely.

AUGUSTE RODIN

You'll find
as you grow older
that you weren't born
such a very great while ago
after all.
The time only shortens up.

WILLIAM DEAN HOWELLS

He was a wise man who said:
"As I grow older
I pay less attention
to what men say.
I just watch
what they do."

WILFRED A. PETERSON

We live in the present,
we dream of the future,
and we learn eternal truths
from the past.

MME. CHIANG KAI-SHEK

It is delightful
to transport one's self
into the spirit of the past,
to see how a wise man
has thought before us,
and to what glorious height
we have at last reached.

JOHANN WOLFGANG VON GOETHE

Education
is a continuous process
ending only
when ambition comes to a halt.

COL. R. I. REES

Every day
increases the sheer weight of knowledge
put into our hands,
some new power control
over natural processes ...
Our age is being forcibly reminded
that knowledge is no substitute
for wisdom.
Far and away
the most important thing
in human life is living it.

FRANK R. BARRY

The man who graduates today
and stops learning tomorrow
is uneducated the day after.

NEWTON D. BAKER

Anyone who stops learning
is old,
whether this happens
at twenty or eighty.
Anyone who keeps on learning
not only remains young,
but becomes constantly more valuable
regardless of physical capacity.

HARVEY ULLMAN

In the advance of civilization,
it is new knowledge
which paves the way,
and the pavement is eternal.

W. R. WHITNEY

Things that I felt absolutely sure of
a few years ago,
I do not believe now;
and this thought
makes me see more clearly
how foolish it would be
to expect all men
to agree with me.

F. D. VAN AMBURGH

The sweetest path of life
leads through the avenues of learning,
and whoever can open up
the way for another,
ought, so far,
to be esteemed a benefactor
to mankind.

DAVID HUME

Get over the idea
that only children
should spend their time in study.
Be a student
so long as you still have
something to learn,
and this will mean all your life.

HENRY L. DOHERTY

EDUCATION

They know enough
who know how to learn.

HENRY ADAMS

Being educated
means to prefer the best
not only to the worst
but to the second best.

WILLIAM LYON PHELPS

Education is no longer thought of
as a preparation for adult life,
but as a continuing process
of growth and development
from birth until death.

STEPHEN MITCHELL

No man can enjoy
the privileges of education
and thereafter with a clear conscience
break his contract with society.

ISAIAH BOWMAN

There is hardly any place
or any company
where you may not gain knowledge,
if you please;
almost everybody
knows some one thing,
and is glad to talk about
that one thing.

LORD CHESTERFIELD

You should have education enough
so that you won't have to look up to people;
and then more education
so that you will be wise enough
not to look down on people.

M. L. BOREN

Perhaps the most valuable result
of all education
is the ability to make yourself
do the thing you have to do
when it has to be done,
whether you like it or not.

HUXLEY

Education today,
more than ever before,
must see clearly
the dual objective:
Educating for living
and educating for making a living.

JAMES MASON WOOD

All who have meditated
on the art of governing mankind
have been convinced
that the fate of empires
depends on the education
of youth.

ARISTOTLE

The young man
who has the combination
of the learning of books
with the learning which comes
of doing things with the hands
need not worry
about getting along in the world today,
or at any time.

WILLIAM S. KNUDSEN

Seeing much, suffering much,
and studying much
are the three pillars of learning.

BENJAMIN DISRAELI

Learning
makes a man fit company
for himself.

YOUNG

Learning without thought
is labor lost;
thought without learning
is perilous.

CONFUCIUS

Jails and prisons
are the complement of schools;
so many less as you
have of the latter,
so many more you
must have of the former.

HORACE MANN

We need an education
in the obvious
more than investigation
of the obscure.

OLIVER WENDELL HOLMES

The great end of education
is, to discipline
rather than to furnish the mind;
to train it to the use of its own powers,
rather than fill it
with the accumulations of others.

TRYON EDWARDS

The two basic processes of education
are knowing and valuing.

ROBERT J. HAVIGHURST

Education is that which remains
when one has forgotten everything
he learned in school.

ALBERT EINSTEIN

EMOTION

Beauty I have learned from the ugly,
charity from the unkind,
and peace from the turmoil of the world.

FREDERICK WARD KATES

———◆◆———

If you have wit,
use it to please and not to hurt:
you may shine like the sun
in the temperate zones
without scorching.

LORD CHESTERFIELD

———◆◆———

We judge of man's wisdom
by his hope.

RALPH WALDO EMERSON

The belief
that youth is the happiest time of life
is founded on a fallacy.
The happiest person
is the person who thinks
the most interesting thoughts
and we grow happier as we grow older.

WILLIAM LYON PHELPS

A fanatic is one
who can't change his mind
and won't change the subject.

WINSTON S. CHURCHILL

It is well for the heart to be naïve
and for the mind not to be.

ANATOLE FRANCE

No true manhood
can be trained
by a merely intellectual process.
You cannot train men
by the intellect alone;
you must train them
by the heart.

JOSEPH PARKER

Know thyself?
If I knew myself,
I'd run away.

JOHANN WOLFGANG VON GOETHE

The mental disease
of the present generation
is impatience of study,
contempt of the great masters
of ancient wisdom,
and a disposition to rely
wholly upon unassisted genius
and natural sagacity.

JOHNSON

Experience has convinced me
that there is a thousand times more goodness,
wisdom, and love in the world
than men imagine.

GEHLES

Life is given for wisdom,
and yet we are not wise;
for goodness,
and we are not good;
for overcoming evil,
and evil remains;
for patience and sympathy and love,
and we are fretful and hard
and weak and selfish.
We are keyed not to attainment,
but to the struggle toward it.

T. T. MUNGER

Knowledge is the eye of desire
and can become
the pilot of the soul.

WILL DURANT

Intellect and industry
are never incompatible.
There is more wisdom,
and will be more benefit,
in combining them
than scholars like to believe,
or than the common world imagine;
life has enough time for both,
and its happiness
will be increased by the union.

S. TURNER

Cleverness
is not wisdom.

EURIPIDES

It takes a clever man
to turn cynic
and a wise man
to be clever enough not to.

FANNIE HURST

———◆◆◆———

He is happy in his wisdom
who has learned
at another's expense.

PLAUTUS

———◆◆◆———

The plainest sign of wisdom
is continual cheerfulness,
her state is like that of things
in the regions above the moon,
always clear and serene.

MICHEL DE MONTAIGNE

EXPERIENCE

Experience takes
dreadfully high school-wages,
but he teaches like no other.

THOMAS CARLYLE

It takes a lot of time
to get experience,
and once you have it
you ought to go on using it.

BENJAMIN M. DUGGAR

The rules which experience suggests
are better than those
which theorists elaborate in their libraries.

RICHARD STORRS

Experience
is the universal mother
of sciences.

MIGUEL DE CERVANTES

———◆———

It is foolish
to try to live on past experience.
It is very dangerous,
if not a fatal habit,
to judge ourselves to be safe
because of something
that we felt or did twenty years ago.

CHARLES SPURGEON

———◆———

The years teach much
which the days never know.

RALPH WALDO EMERSON

He that never changes
his opinions,
never corrects his mistakes,
will never be wiser on the morrow
than he is today.

TRYON EDWARDS

Learn from the mistakes of others—
you can't live long enough
to make them all yourself.

MARTIN VANBEE

Time ripens all things;
no man is born wise.

MIGUEL DE CERVANTES

I have but one lamp
by which my feet are guided,
and that is the lamp
of experience.
I know no way
of judging of the future
but by the past.

PATRICK HENRY

Experience is not
what happens to a man.
It is what a man does
with what happens to him.

ALDOUS HUXLEY

Men are wise in proportion,
not to their experience,
but to their capacity for experience.

GEORGE BERNARD SHAW

The road of excess
leads to the palace of wisdom;
for we never know what is enough
until we know what is more than enough.

WILLIAM BLAKE

I do not think much of a man
who is not wiser today
than he was yesterday.

ABRAHAM LINCOLN

The wisdom of the wise
and the experience of the ages
may be preserved by quotation.

BENJAMIN DISRAELI

There is no merit
where there is no trial;
and till experience stamps
the mark of strength,
cowards may pass for heroes
and faith for falsehood.

AARON HILL

A little experience
often upsets a lot of theory.

CADMAN

To most men
experience is like
the stern lights of a ship,
which illuminate only
the track it has passed.

SAMUEL TAYLOR COLERIDGE

Our experience is composed
rather of illusions lost
than wisdom acquired.

JOSEPH ROUX

Experience is the child of thought,
and thought is the child of action.
We cannot learn men
from books.

BENJAMIN DISRAELI

FAILURE

One who fears failure
limits his activities.
Failure is only the opportunity
more intelligently
to begin again.

HENRY FORD

Many a man
fails to become a thinker
for the sole reason
that his memory is too good.

FRIEDRICH W. NIETZSCHE

There is no such thing
as an inevitable war.
If war comes,
it will be from failure
of human wisdom.

BONAR LAW

We cannot advance
without new experiments in living,
but no wise man
tries every day
what he has proved wrong
the day before.

JAMES TRUSLOW ADAMS

Wisely and slow;
they stumble that run fast.

WILLIAM SHAKESPEARE

What is defeat?
Nothing but education;
nothing but the first step
to something better.

WENDELL PHILLIPS

For everything you have missed
you have gained something else.

RALPH WALDO EMERSON

If you would not have affliction
visit you twice,
listen at once to what it teaches.

JAMES BURGH

Wise men ne'er sit
and wail their loss,
but cheerily seek
how to redress their harms.

WILLIAM SHAKESPEARE

Mistakes
are lessons of wisdom.

HUGH WHITE

Good people are good
because they've
come to wisdom
through failure.

WILLIAM SAROYAN

A man begins cutting
his wisdom teeth
the first time he bites off
more than he can chew.

HERB CAEN

Wisdom is ofttimes nearer
when we stoop
than when we soar.

WILLIAM WORDSWORTH

FOLLY

Very few men
are wise by their own counsel,
or learned by their own teaching;
for he that was only taught by himself
had a fool as his master.

BEN JONSON

For one word
a man is often deemed to be wise,
and for one word
he is often deemed to be foolish.
We should be careful indeed
what we say.

CONFUCIUS

I have always been
among those who believed
that the greatest freedom of speech
was the greatest safety,
because if a man is a fool
the best thing to do
is to encourage him
to advertise the fact by speaking.

WOODROW WILSON

The ultimate result
of shielding men
from the effects of folly
is to fill the world with fools.

HERBERT SPENCER

Much of the wisdom
of one age
is the folly of the next.

CHARLES SIMMONS

Experiment is folly
when experience
shows the way.

ROGER BABSON

He who lives
without folly
is not so wise
as he thinks.

FRANÇOIS LA ROCHEFOUCAULD

Wisdom

is the right use of knowledge.
To know is not to be wise.
Many men know a great deal,
and are all the greater fools for it.
There is no fool so great a fool
as a knowing fool.
But to know how to use knowledge
is to have wisdom.

SPURGEON

Politeness

is not always the sign of wisdom,
but the want of it always leaves suspicion
for folly.

WALTER SAVAGE LANDOR

Men who know themselves
are no longer fools;
they stand on the threshhold
of the Door of Wisdom.

HAVELOCK ELLIS

Fool me once,
shame on you;
fool me twice,
shame on me.

CHINESE PROVERB

No man
really becomes a fool
until he stops asking questions.

CHARLES P. STEINMETZ

The man who questions opinion
is wise;
the man who quarrels with fact
is a fool.

FRANK A. GARBUTT

A wise man
gets more out of his enemies
than a fool
gets out of his friends.

BALTASAR GRACIÁN

One great difference
between a wise man and a fool is,
the former only wishes
for what he may possibly obtain;
the latter desires impossibilities.

DEMOCRITUS

If one's life reaches
to or beyond seventy,
one must have acquired some wisdom
along the way
or be intellectually dead
or a damned fool.

DOROTHY MCCALL

He dares to be a fool,
and that is
the first step in the direction
of wisdom.

JAMES GIBBONS HUNEKER

FREEDOM

The revelation of thought
takes man out of servitude
into freedom.

RALPH WALDO EMERSON

He who has no opinion of his own,
but depends upon the opinion
and taste of others,
is a slave.

FRIEDRICH KLOPSTOCK

Democracy needs more free speech,
for even the speech
of foolish people is valuable
if it serves to guarantee
the right of the wise to talk.

DAVID CUSHMAN COYLE

Without freedom of thought,
there can be no such thing
as wisdom.

BENJAMIN FRANKLIN

The people never give up their liberties
but under some delusion.

EDMUND BURKE

None are more hopelessly enslaved
than those who falsely believe
they are free.

JOHANN WOLFGANG VON GOETHE

Citizens may be born free;
they are not born wise.
Therefore, the business of liberal education
in a democracy
is to make free men wise.

F. CHAMPION WARD

Thinking is one thing
no one has ever been able to tax.

CHARLES F. KETTERING

All free governments
are managed by the combined wisdom and folly
of the people.

JAMES A. GARFIELD

No army can withstand the strength
of an idea whose time has come.

VICTOR HUGO

Intellect annuls fate.
So far as a man
thinks he is free.

RALPH WALDO EMERSON

Real freedom
comes from the mastery,
through knowledge,
of historic conditions and race character,
which makes possible
a free and intelligent use of experience
for the purpose of progress.

HAMILTON WRIGHT MABIE

Education
is the cheap defense
of nations.

EDMUND BURKE

Thought is the first faculty of man;
to express it is one of his first desires;
to spread it, his dearest privilege.

ABBÉ RAYNAL

Where wisdom is called for,
force is of little use.

HERODOTUS

The war for freedom
will never really be won
because the price of freedom
is constant vigilance over ourselves
and over our Government.

ELEANOR ROOSEVELT

Perfect freedom is as necessary
to the health and vigor of commerce
as it is to the health and vigor of citizenship.

PATRICK HENRY

One should never put on
one's best trousers
to go out to fight for freedom.

HENRIK IBSEN

When perfect sincerity is expected,
perfect freedom must be allowed.

TACITUS

A splendid storehouse
of integrity and freedom
has been bequeathed to us
by our forefathers.
In this day of confusion,
of peril to liberty,
our high duty is
to see that this storehouse
is not robbed of its contents.

HERBERT HOOVER

GENIUS

Man's brain is, after all,
the greatest natural resource.

KARL BRANDT

———

Genius is only
a superior power of seeing.

JOHN RUSKIN

———

When a true genius
appears in the world,
you may know him by this sign,
that the dunces
are all in confederacy against him.

JONATHAN SWIFT

Times of general calamity
and confusion
have ever been productive
of the greatest minds.
The purest ore
is produced from the hottest furnace,
and the brightest thunderbolt
is elicited from the darkest storm.

CHARLES CALEB COLTON

Every production of genius
must be the production
of enthusiasm.

BENJAMIN DISRAELI

Great geniuses
have the shortest biographies.

RALPH WALDO EMERSON

The mind's the standard
of the man.

WATTS

One of the strongest characteristics of genius
is the power of lighting its own fire.

JOHN FOSTER

A small mind
is obstinate.
A great mind
can lead and be led.

ALEXANDER CANNON

Genius
is eternal patience.

MICHELANGELO

On earth
there is nothing great but man;
in man there is nothing great
but mind.

SIR WILLIAM HAMILTON

The intellect of the wise
is like glass:
It admits the light of heaven
and reflects it.

AUGUSTUS HARE

Be wisely worldly,
but not worldly wise.

FRANCIS QUARLES

Wisdom is special knowledge
in excess of all that is known.

AMBROSE BIERCE

Great minds have purposes,
others have wishes.

WASHINGTON IRVING

*I*GNORANCE

Facts do not cease to exist
because they are ignored.

ALDOUS HUXLEY

To admit ignorance
is to exhibit wisdom.

ASHLEY MONTAGU

Half-knowledge
is worse than ignorance.

THOMAS B. MACAULAY

To be ignorant of the lives
of the most celebrated men of antiquity
is to continue in a state of childhood
all our days.

PLUTARCH

A great idea is usually original
to more than one discoverer.
Great ideas come
when the world needs them.
They surround the world's ignorance
and press for admission.

AUSTIN PHELPS

There is no darkness—
but ignorance.

WILLIAM SHAKESPEARE

A man is never astonished
that he doesn't know what another does,
but he is surprised
at the gross ignorance of the other
not knowing what he does.

THOMAS CHANDLER HALIBURTON

The best part of our knowledge
is that which teaches us
where knowledge leaves off
and ignorance begins.

OLIVER WENDELL HOLMES

Knowledge and human power
are synonymous,
since the ignorance of the cause
frustrates the effect.

FRANCIS BACON

The recipe for perpetual ignorance is:
Be satisfied with your opinions
and content with your knowledge.

ELBERT HUBBARD

It is well for people who think
to change their minds occasionally
in order to keep them clean.
For those who do not think,
it is best at least
to rearrange their prejudices.

LUTHER BURBANK

A vacant mind
invites dangerous inmates.

NICHOLAS HILLIARD

The wise person possesses humility.
He knows that his small island of knowledge
is surrounded by a vast sea
of the unknown.

HAROLD C. CHASE

The chief aim of wisdom
is to enable one to bear with
the stupidity of the ignorant.

WINSTON S. CHURCHILL

Ignorance of all things
is an evil neither terrible nor excessive,
nor yet the greatest of all;
but great cleverness and much learning,
if they be accompanied
by a bad training,
are a much greater misfortune.

PLATO

INGENUITY

Every great advance
in science
has issued from a new audacity
of imagination.

JOHN DEWEY

Words are often seen
hunting for an idea,
but ideas are never seen
hunting for words.

H. W. SHAW

Action without study
is fatal.
Study without action
is futile.

MARY BEARD

Dare to be wise; begin!
He who postpones
the hour of living rightly
is like the rustic
who waits for the river to run out
before he crosses.

HORACE

———

Whoever acquires knowledge
but does not practice it
is as one who ploughs
but does not sow.

SAADI

———

'Now' is the watchword
of the wise.

CHARLES H. SPURGEON

The saying that knowledge is power
is not quite true.
Used knowledge is power,
and more than power.
It is money, and service,
and better living for our fellowmen,
and a hundred other good things.
But mere knowledge, left unused,
has no power in it.

EDWARD E. FREE

All men see the same objects,
but do not equally understand them.
Intelligence is the tongue
that discerns and tastes them.

THOMAS TRAHERNE

Real intelligence
is a creative use of knowledge,
not merely an accumulation
of facts.

D. KENNETH WINEBRENNER

Getting an idea
should be like sitting down on a pin;
it should make you jump up
and do something.

E. L. SIMPSON

He is great
who can do what he wishes;
he is wise
who wishes to do what he can.

AUGUST IFFLAND

A wise man will make tools
of what comes to hand.

THOMAS FULLER

A wise man
will make more opportunities
than he finds.

FRANCIS BACON

Wisdom denotes
the pursuing of the best ends
by the best means.

FRANCES HUTCHESON

Nine-tenths of wisdom
consists in being wise
in time.

THEODORE ROOSEVELT

INSPIRATION

If you make people
think they're thinking,
they'll love you.
If you really make them think,
they'll hate you.

DON MARQUIS

A room hung with pictures
is a room hung with thoughts.

JOSHUA REYNOLDS

A moment's insight is sometimes
worth a life's experience.

OLIVER WENDELL HOLMES

A good idea
that is not shared with others
will gradually fade away
and bear no fruit,
but when it is shared
it lives forever
because it is passed on
from one person to another
and grows as it goes.

LOWELL FILLMORE

A thought
may be very commendable
as a thought,
but I value it chiefly
as a window
through which I can obtain
insight on the thinker.

ALEXANDER SMITH

Your most brilliant ideas
come in a flash,
but the flash comes
only after a lot of hard work.
Nobody gets a big idea
when he is not relaxed
and nobody gets a big idea
when he is relaxed all the time.

EDWARD BLAKESLEE

Each thought
that is welcomed and recorded
is a nest egg,
by the side of which
more will be laid.

HENRY DAVID THOREAU

The aim of education
should be to convert the mind
into a living fountain,
and not a reservoir.
That which is filled
by merely pumping in,
will be emptied by pumping out.

JOHN·M. MASON

What a man knows
should find expression
in what he does.
The chief value
of superior knowledge
is that it leads
to a performing manhood.

CHRISTIAN BOVEE

The inlet of a man's mind
is what he learns;
the outlet
is what he accomplishes.
If his mind is not fed
by a continued supply of new ideas
which he puts to work with purpose,
and if there is no outlet in action,
his mind becomes stagnant.
Such a mind is a danger
to the individual who owns it
and is useless to the community.

JEREMIAH W. JENKS

From the little spark
may burst a mighty flame.

DANTE

The best teacher
is the one who suggests
rather than dogmatizes,
and inspires his listener
with the wish to teach himself.

BULWER

A man would do well
to carry a pencil in his pocket,
and write down the thoughts
of the moment.
Those that come unsought for
are commonly the most valuable,
and should be secured,
because they seldom return.

FRANCIS BACON

Many ideas grow better
when transplanted
into another mind
than in the one
where they sprang up.

OLIVER WENDELL HOLMES

Ideas are
the mightiest influence
on earth.
One great thought
breathed into a man
may regenerate him.

CHANNING

The gates of thought,
— how slow and late they discover themselves!
Yet when they appear,
we see that they were always there,
always open.

RALPH WALDO EMERSON

A fresh mind
keeps the body fresh.
Take in the ideas of the day,
drain off those of yesterday.
As to the morrow,
time enough to consider it
when it becomes today.

BULWER

Ideas lose themselves
as quickly as quail,
and one must wing them
the minute they
rise out of the grass—
or they are gone.

THOMAS F. KENNEDY

‘

JUDGMENT

The two powers
which in my opinion
constitute a wise man
are those of bearing
and forbearing.

EPICTETUS

A right judgment
draws us a profit
from all things we see.

WILLIAM SHAKESPEARE

What we do not understand
we have no right to judge.

HENRI FRÉDÉRIC AMIEL

Often a dash
of judgment
is better
than a flash of genius.

HOWARD W. NEWTON

A prudent question
is one-half of wisdom.

FRANCIS BACON

Associate with men of judgment,
for judgment is found
in conversation,
and we make another man's judgment ours
by frequenting his company.

THOMAS FULLER

Knowledge comes,
but wisdom lingers.
It may not be difficult
to store up in the mind
a vast quantity of facts
within a comparatively short time,
but the ability to form judgments
requires the severe discipline
of hard work
and the tempering heat
of experience and maturity.

CALVIN COOLIDGE

Wisdom is knowing
when to speak your mind
and when to mind your speech.

EVANGEL

An open mind
is all very well in its way,
but it ought not to be so open
that there is no keeping anything
in or out of it.
It should be capable
of shutting its doors sometimes,
or it may be found a little draughty.

SAMUEL BUTLER

To live is not to learn,
but to apply.

LEGOUVÉ

The whole object of education is,
or should be,
to develop mind.
The mind should be a thing
that works.
It should be able to pass judgment
on events as they arise,
make decisions.

SHERWOOD ANDERSON

In some small field
each child should attain,
within the limited range
of its experience and observation,
the power to draw
a justly limited inference
from observed facts.

CHARLES W. ELIOT

Each excellent thing,
once learned,
serves for a measure
of all other knowledge.

SIR P. SIDNEY

Is anyone educated
in whom the powers
of conscious reasoning
are untrained or undeveloped,
however great may be the store
of accumulated knowledge?

JOSEPH H. ODELL

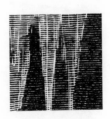

Judgment of the people
is often wiser
than the wisest men.

LAJOS KOSSUTH

A wise man
sees as much as he ought,
not as much as he can.

MICHEL DE MONTAIGNE

The wise man
sees in the misfortunes of others
what he should avoid.

SYRUS

PRINCIPLE

A man is not idle
because he is absorbed in thought.
There is a visible labor
and there is an invisible labor.

VICTOR HUGO

Minds are like parachutes—
they only function when open.

THOMAS DEWAR

Most men believe
that it would benefit them
if they could get a little
from those who have more.
How much more would it benefit them
if they would learn a little
from those who know more.

WILLIAM J. H. BOETCKER

It is the hardest thing in the world
to be a good thinker
without being a good self examiner.

LORD SHAFTESBURY

The wise man
does not expose himself needlessly
to danger,
since there are few things
for which he cares sufficiently;
but he is willing, in great crises
to give even his life—
knowing that under certain conditions
it is not worthwhile to live.

ARISTOTLE

Thought, not money,
is the real business capital,
and if you know absolutely
that what you are doing is right,
then you are bound
to accomplish it in due season.

HARVEY FIRESTONE

The one and only
formative power given to man
is thought.
By thinking
he not only makes character,
but body and affairs,
for "as he thinketh within himself,
so is he."

CHARLES FILLMORE

The price of wisdom
is eternal thought.

FRANK BIRCH

Education
is the process by which
the individual relates himself
to the universe,
gives himself citizenship
in the changing world,
shares the race's mind
and enfranchises his own soul.

JOHN H. FINLEY

Life is a mirror
and will reflect back
to the thinker
what he thinks into it.

ERNEST HOLMES

Merely having an open mind
is nothing.
The object of opening the mind,
as of opening the mouth,
is to shut it again on something solid.

GILBERT K. CHESTERTON

A grain of knowledge,
of genuine controllable conviction,
will outweigh a bushel of adroitness.

JOHN SEELEY

There will always be
a Frontier
where there
is an open mind
and a willing hand.

CHARLES F. KETTERING

Thinking well is wise;
planning well, wiser;
doing well
wisest and best of all.

PERSIAN PROVERB

Thinking
without constructive
action becomes a disease.

HENRY FORD

He is a wise man
who wastes no energy
on pursuits for which he is not fitted,
and he is still wiser who,
from among the things that he can do well,
chooses and resolutely follows the best.

WILLIAM E. GLADSTONE

Wisdom is knowing
what to do next,
virtue is doing it.

DAVID STARR JORDAN

RESPONSIBILITY

Wisdom, itself,
is often an abstraction
associated not with fact or reality,
but with the man
who asserts it
and the manner of its assertion.

JOHN KENNETH GALBRAITH

Teach the young people
how to think,
not what to think.

SIDNEY SUGARMAN

The biggest problem
in the world
could have been solved
when it was small.

WITTER BYNNER

Better three hours too early,
than one minute too late.

WILLIAM SHAKESPEARE

The most valuable result of education
is the ability to make yourself do
the thing you ought to do
when it ought to be done,
whether you have to do it or not.

THOMAS H. HUXLEY

A man should never be ashamed
to own he has been in the wrong,
which is but saying in other words,
that he is wiser today
than he was yesterday.

ALEXANDER POPE

He who is taught
to live upon little
owes more to his father's wisdom
than he who has a great deal left him
does to his father's care.

WILLIAM PENN

The only way
in which one human being
can properly attempt
to influence another
is by encouraging him
to think for himself,
instead of endeavoring
to instill
ready-made opinions
into his head.

LESLIE STEPHEN

The habit of saving
is itself an education;
it fosters every virtue,
teaches self-denial,
cultivates the sense of order,
trains to forethought,
and so broadens the mind.

T. T. MUNGER

Knowledge of our duties
is the most essential part
of the philosophy of life.
If you escape duty
you avoid action.
The world demands results.

GEORGE W. GOETHALS

Education is a debt
due from the present
to the future generations.

GEORGE PEABODY

The wisest
have the most authority.

PLATO

If we are not responsible
for the thoughts that
pass our doors,
we are at least responsible
for those we admit and entertain.

CHARLES B. NEWCOMB

You can't escape
the responsibility of tomorrow
by evading it today.

ABRAHAM LINCOLN

———————

The wise man must remember
that while he is a descendant
of the past,
he is a parent of the future.

HERBERT SPENCER

What is strength
without a double share
of wisdom?
Strength's not made to rule,
but to subserve,
where wisdom bears command.

JOHN MILTON

RHETORIC

By words
we learn thoughts,
and by thoughts
we learn life.

JEAN BAPTISTE GIRARD

Brisk talkers
are usually slow thinkers.
There is, indeed,
no wild beast
more to be dreaded
than a communicative man
having nothing to communicate.

JONATHAN SWIFT

What you keep by you,
you may change and mend;
but words, once spoken,
can never be recalled.

WENTWORTH ROSCOMMON

When I'm getting ready
to reason with a man,
I spend one-third of my time
thinking about myself
and what I am going to say—
and two-thirds thinking about him
and what he is going to say.

ABRAHAM LINCOLN

There is no calamity
that right words will not begin to redress.

RALPH WALDO EMERSON

It is not enough
to harvest knowledge by study;
the wind of talk
must winnow it
and blow away the chaff.
Then will the clear,
bright grains of wisdom
be garnered,
for our own use
or that of others.

WILLIAM MATTHEWS

———

Colors fade,
temples crumble,
empires fall,
but wise words endure.

THORNDIKE

One great use of words
is to hide our thoughts.

FRANÇOIS-MARIE AROUET VOLTAIRE

Speech is the gift of all,
but thought of few.

CATO

A single conversation across the table
with a wise man
is worth a month's study of books.

CHINESE PROVERB

Thinking
is the talking of the soul
with itself.

PLATO

Sleep not
when others speak,
sit not when others stand,
speak not
when you should hold your peace,
walk not when others stop.

GEORGE WASHINGTON

Much wisdom
often goes with little words.

SOPHOCLES

SENSE

The wise man
thinks about his troubles
only when there is some purpose
in doing so;
at other times
he thinks about other things.

BERTRAND RUSSELL

⸻

It is curious
how tyrannical the habit
of reading is,
and what shifts we make
to escape thinking.
There is no bore we dread
being left alone with
so much as our own minds.

JAMES RUSSELL LOWELL

All the problems of the world
could be settled easily
if men were only willing to think.

NICHOLAS MURRAY BUTLER

I find
that a great part of the information I have
was acquired
by looking up something
and finding something else
on the way.

FRANKLIN P. ADAMS

Wisdom is to the mind
what health is to the body.

FRANÇOIS LA ROCHEFOUCAULD

Let us not dream
that reason can ever be popular.
Passions, emotions,
may be made popular,
but reason remains ever
the property of the few.

JOHANN WOLFGANG VON GOETHE

Knowledge comes
by taking things apart: analysis.
But wisdom comes
by putting things together.

JOHN A. MORRISON

It is a thousand times better
to have common sense without education
than to have education
without common sense.

ROBERT G. INGERSOLL

Common sense
in an uncommon degree
is what the world calls wisdom.

SAMUEL TAYLOR COLERIDGE

⸻

When a man's knowledge
is not in order,
the more of it he has
the greater will be his confusion.

HERBERT SPENCER

⸻

One pound of learning
requires ten pounds of common sense
to apply it.

PERSIAN PROVERB

Common sense
is the knack of seeing things
as they are,
and doing things
as they ought to be done.

STOWE

Second thoughts
are ever wiser.

EURIPIDES

Common sense
is the favorite daughter
of reason.

H. W. SHAW

Wisdom consists
in rising superior
both to madness
and to common sense,
and is lending oneself
to the universal illusion
without becoming its dupe.

HENRI FRÉDÉRIC AMIEL

Where is the wisdom
we have lost in knowledge?

T. S. ELIOT

The wisdom of the wise
is an uncommon degree
of common sense.

WILLIAM RALPH INGE

Any fool can tell the truth,
but it requires a man
of some sense
to know how to lie well.

SAMUEL BUTLER

SYMPATHY

One age
cannot be completely understood
if all the others are not understood.
The song of history
can only be sung as a whole.

JOSÉ ORTEGA Y GASSET

No matter how widely
you have traveled,
you haven't seen the world
if you have failed to look
into the human hearts
that inhabit it.

DONALD C. PEATTIE

If we have not peace
within ourselves,
it is in vain
to seek it
from outward sources.

FRANÇOIS LA ROCHEFOUCAULD

Thoughts are wonderful things,
that they can bring two people,
so far apart,
into harmony and understanding
for even a little while.

ERNEST PYLE

If you wish to please people,
you must
begin by understanding them.

CHARLES READE

Peace comes only from loving,
from mutual self-sacrifice
and self-forgetfulness.
Few today have humility
or wisdom enough
to know the world's
deep need of love.
We are too much possessed
by national and racial
and cultural pride.

HORACE W. B. DONEGAN

Wisdom is the power
that enables us to use knowledge
for the benefit of ourselves
and others.

THOMAS J. WATSON

Consideration
is not merely a matter
of emotional goodwill
but of intellectual vigor
and moral self-sacrifice.
Wisdom must combine
with sympathy.

CHARLES SEYMOUR

Sympathy
is a thing to be encouraged
apart from humane considerations,
because it supplies us
with the materials for wisdom.

ROBERT LOUIS STEVENSON

In the deep, unwritten
wisdom of life
there are many things
to be learned
that cannot be taught.
We never know them
by hearing them spoken,
but we grow into them
by experience
and recognize them
through understanding.
Understanding
is a great experience in itself,
but it does not come
through instruction.

ANTHONY HOPE

Suffering becomes beautiful
when anyone bears great calamities
with cheerfulness,
not through insensibility
but through greatness of mind.

ARISTOTLE

⟡

Keep me away
from the wisdom
which does not cry,
the philosophy
which does not laugh
and the greatest
which does not bow
before children.

KAHLIL GIBRAN

True wisdom
comes from the overcoming
of suffering and sin.
All true wisdom
is therefore touched
with sadness.

WHITTAKER CHAMBERS

All wisdom
may be reduced to two words—
wait and hope.

ALEXANDRE DUMAS

Perhaps wisdom
is to be found in people
who have suffered greatly
but have surmounted it.

LOUIS JOLYON WEST

TRUTH

The pursuit of truth
shall set you free—
even if you never catch up with it.

CLARENCE DARROW

Falsehood
is never so successful
as when she baits her hook
with truth,
and no opinions
so fatally mislead us
as those that are not wholly wrong.

CHARLES CALEB COLTON

We must not let go
manifest truths
because we cannot answer
all questions about them.

JEREMY COLLIER

Much of truth
is found upon the battlefield
of controversy,
and it is kept alive
by sharp exchanges.

LAWRENCE A. KIMPTON

Every man
who expresses an honest thought
is a soldier
in the army of intellectual liberty.

ROBERT G. INGERSOLL

The greatest truths
are the simplest;
and so are the greatest men.

JULIUS C. HARE

Some men's words
I remember so well
that I must often use them
to express my thought.
Yes, because I perceive
that we have heard the same truth,
but they have heard it better.

RALPH WALDO EMERSON

Cynics and critics
wake us up.
Kindness often covers up the truth
and allows us to sleep on
in our ignorance.

WILFRED A. PETERSON

There is no wisdom
like frankness.

BENJAMIN DISRAELI

It is the calling of great men,
not so much to preach new truths,
as to rescue from oblivion
those old truths
which it is our wisdom to remember
and our weakness to forget.

SIDNEY SMITH

There is no wisdom
save in truth.
Truth is everlasting,
but our ideas about truth
are changeable.
Only a little
of the first fruits of wisdom,
only a few fragments
of the boundless heights,
breadths and depths of truth,
have I been able to gather.

MARTIN LUTHER

It is well
when the wise and the learned
discover new truths;
but how much better
to diffuse the truths already known
amongst the multitudes.

HORACE MANN

He that would make real progress
in knowledge
must dedicate his age
as well as youth,
the latter growth
as well as the first fruits,
at the altar of truth.

BERKELEY

The first point of wisdom
is to discern that which is false;
the second to know that which is true.

LACTANIUS

The use of traveling
is to regulate imagination by reality, and,
instead of thinking how things may be,
to see them as they are.

JOHNSON

Adams, Franklin P., 129
Adams, Henry, 24
Adams, James Truslow, 49
Amiel, Henri Frédéric, 98, 133
Anderson, Sherwood, 102
Aristophanes, 13
Aristotle, 27, 107, 141

Babson, Roger, 56
Bacon, Francis, 4, 78, 86, 93, 99
Baker, Newton D., 19
Barry, Frank R., 19
Beard, Mary, 82
Berkeley, 149
Bierce, Ambrose, 74
Birch, Frank, 109
Blake, William, 44
Blakeslee, Edward, 90
Boetcker, William J. H., 106
Boren, M. L., 26
Bovee, Christian, 91
Bowman, Isaiah, 25
Brandt, Karl, 70
Buddha, 12
Bulwer, 93, 95
Bunche, Ralph J., 13
Burbank, Luther, 79
Burgh, James, 50
Burke, Edmund, 63, 66
Butler, Nicholas Murray, 129
Butler, Samuel, 101, 134
Bynner, Witter, 114
Byrd, Richard E., 8

Cadman, 45
Caen, Herb, 52
Cannon, Alexander, 72
Carlyle, Thomas, 40
Cato, 125
Chambers, Whittaker, 142
Channing, 94
Chase, Harold C., 80
Chesterfield, Lord, 2, 25, 32
Chesterton, Gilbert K., 110
Churchill, Winston S., 33, 80

Coleridge, Samuel Taylor, 46, 131
Collier, Jeremy, 145
Collins, Churton, 2
Colton, Charles Caleb, 71, 144
Confucius, 29, 54
Coolidge, Calvin, 100
Coyle, David Cushman, 62

Dante, 92
Darrow, Clarence, 144
de Cervantes, Miguel, 41, 42
de Montaigne, Michel, 38, 104
Defoe, Daniel, 9
Democritus, 59
Dewar, Thomas, 106
Dewey, John, 82
Diderot, Denis, 9
Disraeli, Benjamin, 28, 45, 46, 71, 147
Doherty, Henry L., 22
Donegan, Horace W. B., 138
Dresser, H. W., 8
Duggar, Benjamin M., 40
Dumas, Alexander, 142
Durant, Will, 36

Edwards, Tryon, 30, 42
Einstein, Albert, 30
Eliot, Charles W., 102
Eliot, T. S., 133
Ellis, Havelock, 58
Emerson, Ralph Waldo, 32, 41, 50, 62, 65, 71, 95, 123, 146
Epictetus, 98
Euripides, 14, 37, 132
Evangel, 101

Fillmore, Charles, 108
Fillmore, Lowell, 89
Finley, John H., 109
Firestone, Harvey, 108
Ford, Henry, 48, 112
Foster, John, 72
France, Anatole, 34
Franklin, Benjamin, 11, 63

Free, Edward E., 84
Fuller, Thomas, 86, 99
Galbraith, John Kenneth, 114
Garbutt, Frank A., 59
Garfield, James A., 64
Gehles, 35
Gibran, Kahlil, 141
Girard, Jean Baptiste, 122
Gladstone, William E., 112
Goethals, George W., 117
Gracián, Baltasar, 3, 5, 59

Haliburton, Thomas Chandler, 78
Hamilton, Sir William, 73
Hare, Augustus, 73
Hare, Julius C. , 146
Havighurst, Robert J., 30
Heinlein, Robert A., 6
Helvetius, 6
Henry, Patrick, 43, 67
Herodotus, 66
Hill, Aaron, 45
Hilliard, Nicholas, 79
Hobbes, Thomas, 11
Holmes, Ernest, 110
Holmes, Oliver Wendell, 29, 78, 88, 94
Hoover, Herbert, 68
Hope, Anthony, 140
Horace, 83
Howells, William Dean, 16
Hubbard, Elbert, 79
Hugo, Victor, 65, 106
Hume, David, 21
Huneker, James Gibbons, 60
Hurst, Fannie, 38
Hutcheson, Frances, 86
Huxley, 26
Huxley, Aldous, 43, 76
Huxley, Thomas H., 115

Ibsen, Henrik, 67
Iffland, August, 85
Inge, William Ralph, 134
Ingersoll, Robert G., 130, 145
Irving, Washington, 74

INDEX

Jenks, Jeremiah W., 92
Johnson, 35, 150
Jonson, Ben, 54
Jordan, David Starr, 112

Kai-Shek, Mme. Chiang, 17
Kates, Frederick Ward, 32
Kennedy, Thomas F., 96
Kettering, Charles F., 64, 111
Kimpton, Lawrence A., 145
Klopstock, Friedrich, 62
Knudsen, William S., 28
Kossuth, Lajos, 104

La Rouchefoucauld, François, 56, 129, 137
Lactanius, 150
Landor, Walter Savage, 57
Law, Bonar, 49
Legouvé, 101
Lincoln, Abraham, 44, 119, 123
Lowell, James Russell, 128
Luther, Martin, 148

Mabie, Hamilton Wright, 65
Macaulay, Thomas B., 76
Mann, Horace, 29, 149
Marquis, Don, 88
Mason, John M., 91
Matthews, William, 124
McCall, Dorothy, 60
Michelangelo, 72
Milton, John, 120
Mitchell, Stephen, 24
Montagu, Ashley, 76
Morrison, John A., 130
Munger, T. T., 36, 117

Newcomb, Charles B., 118
Newton, Howard W., 99
Nietzsche, Friedrich W., 13, 48

O'Shea, 10
Odell, Joseph H., 103
Ortega Y Gasset, José, 136

Parker, Joseph, 34
Peabody, A. P., 10
Peabody, George, 118
Peattie, Donald C., 136
Pecora, Ferdinand, 3
Penn, William, 116
Peterson, Wilfred A., 17, 147
Phelps, Austin, 77
Phelps, William Lyon, 24, 33
Phillips, Wendell, 50
Plato, 11, 80, 118, 125
Plautus, 38
Plutarch, 77
Pope, Alexander, 115
Proverbs
    Chinese, 58, 125
    Persian, 111, 131
Pyle, Ernest, 137

Quarles, Francis, 73

Raynal, Abbé, 66
Reade, Charles, 137
Rees, Col. R. I., 18
Reynolds, Joshua, 88
Rodin, Auguste, 16
Roosevelt, Eleanor, 67
Roosevelt, Theodore, 86
Roscommon, Wentworth, 123
Ross, Galen Starr, 10
Roux, Joseph, 46
Ruskin, John, 70
Russell, Bertrand, 128

Saadi, 83
Saroyan, William, 51
Seabury, David, 3
Seeley, John, 111
Seymour, Charles, 139
Shaftesbury, Lord, 107
Shakespeare, William, 9, 49, 51, 77, 98, 115
Shaw, George Bernard, 44
Shaw, H. W., 82, 132
Sidney, Sir P., 103
Simmons, Charles, 56
Simpson, E. L., 85
Smith, Alexander, 89

Smith, Sidney, 147
Sophocles, 126
Sparks, Jared, 2
Spencer, Herbert, 55, 119, 131
Spurgeon, 57
Spurgeon, Charles, 41, 83
Steinmetz, Charles P., 58
Stephen, Leslie, 116
Stevenson, Robert Louis, 139
Storrs, Richard, 40
Stowe, 132
Sugarman, Sidney, 114
Swift, Jonathan, 12, 70, 122
Syrus, 5, 104

Tacitus, 12, 68
Thoreau, Henry David, 90
Thorndike, 124
Tolstoi, Leo, 16
Traherne, Thomas, 84
Turner, S., 37

Ullman, Harvey, 20

Van Amburgh, F. D., 21
Vanbee, Martin, 42
Voltaire, François-Marie Arouet, 125
Von Goethe, Johann Wolfgang, 5, 6, 18, 34, 63, 130
Von Schiller, Friedrich, 6

Ward, F. Champion, 64
Washington, George, 126
Watson, Thomas J., 138
Watts, 72
West, Louis Jolyon, 142
White, Hugh, 51
Whitman, Walt, 4
Whitney, W. R., 20
Wilson, Woodrow, 5, 55
Winebrenner, D. Kenneth, 85
Wood, James Mason, 27
Wordsworth, William, 52

Young, 28